for Jake,

⌐0 Lovers
to Make
and Do

Brother in
south London –
collage mentality
Sophie Herxheimer
x

Sophie
Herxheimer

Henningham Family Press | London | 2019

GW00642978

First published in 2019 by Henningham Family Press
130 Sandringham Road, London, E8 2HJ
henninghamfamilypress.co.uk
@HenninghamPress

Printed and bound by T.J. International Ltd, Padstow
& Henningham Family Press, London

ISBN   9781999797478
ARTISTS' BOOK (henninghamfamilypress.co.uk)

Supported using public funding by
**ARTS COUNCIL
ENGLAND**
LOTTERY FUNDED

Make

Collect together

Tea plate
Pencil
Needle
Cotton
Material
Kapok.

Now join:

Dra   circ
mate   . 'C
it at   end
edg   the
sti   tightly
m

60 Lovers
to Make
and Do

**Sophie
Herxheimer**

Henningham Family Press

for Adam
who thought
god is real

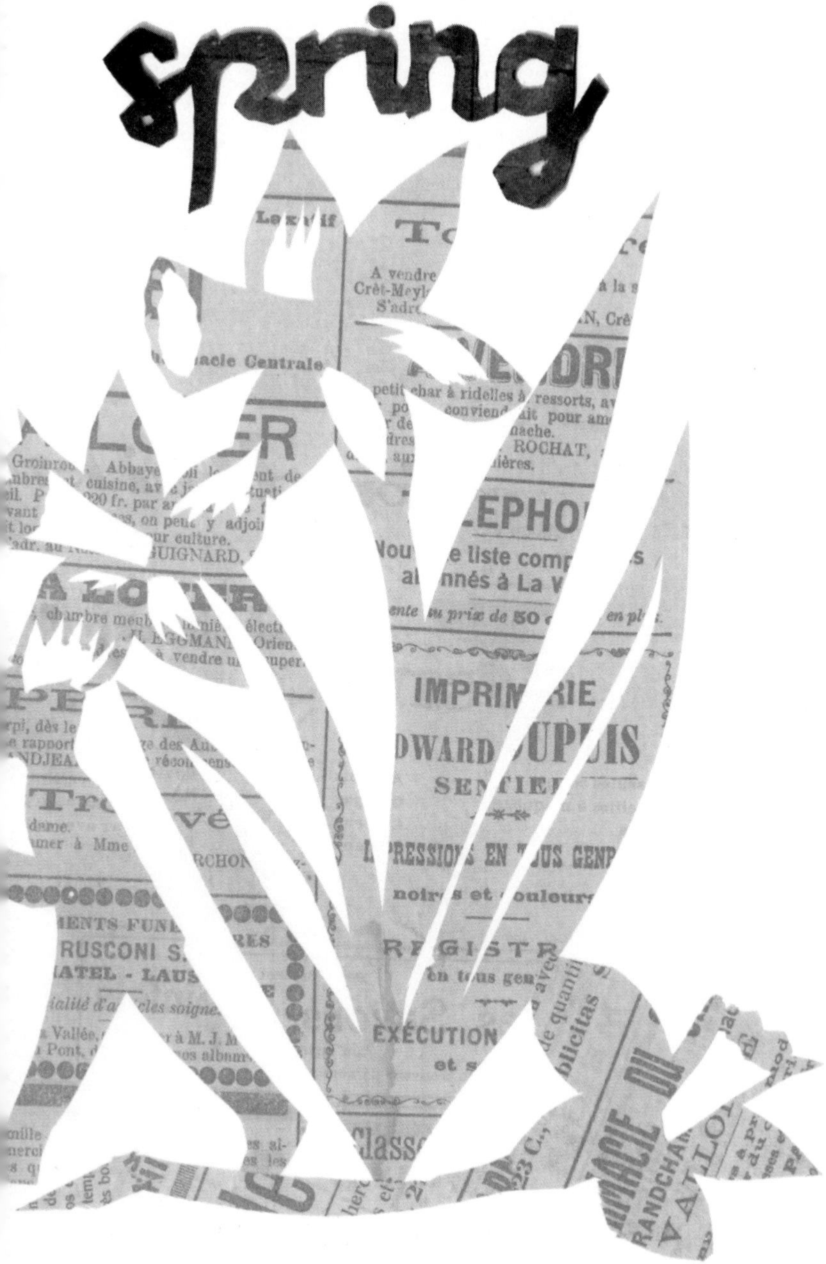
spring

ELIZABETHAN CUP AND COVER.
1585.

Silver-gilt. Height 10¼ in.

ELIZABETHAN STONEWARE JUG,
c. 1570.

With silver-mounted cover and foot.

(*By courtesy of Messrs. Crichton Brothers.*)

95

Undertaker

She spirited a suitor from incense, nail clippings
   and some ceramic tiles.
She kept him in a coffin to start with
but he was so quiet and respectful
she invited him home to live with her.
Her parents never knew about him,
   well they do now.

Barista

She conjured a lover from a SIM card
   and a stack of flyers for local gigs,
he loved to watch her tamp the grinds
twist the group handle, steam milk
to double its height and slowly circle it
as heavy froth, rhythmically filling
and mounding the cup
with downy narcotic snow.
   Chocolate on top? he'd tease her later,
catching her capable hands
and licking her glazed upturned cups
in their perfumed afternoon.

Historian

She traced a lover from shards of bone china
and a wallet of faded letters
  scrawled in extravagant loops.
A wasp-waisted woman in tattered satins
flew into her bed like heaven,
blushed, put her dainty hand straight
on her authenticator's vagina.
  Murmuring, they slowly unpicked
each other's knotty lacings and stiff braids
and spent the next several years
loosening and shuddering
their hair and the truth
about their long separated centuries.

Poet

She drafted a lover from garden spiders,
jumble sale table-linen and gratings from
   her late grandmother's lavender soap.
Languorous, delicate and long-winded,
he unfurled himself like jasmine petals in
a glass teapot and lay next to her,
whispering his poetry, which he interspersed
with surprising gales of laughter.
   He seemed to find her rough peasanty legs
and coarse facial features very amusing.

Confectioner

She sculpted a lover from marzipan
flipped the sign on the door from open to closed
stared long and hard at her handiwork
snuck two dainty bites from the back of his neck.
The almond night fell about them like lace.

Life Coach

She fashioned a lover from smooth
    beach pebbles, a map of Paris and some Cif.
This lover was a large capable blonde woman
in tight jeans who winked and professed love
the very second she appeared.
she was the best thing since
and also a bit like, sliced bread.

ith counter arches in each of the openings were put
alize the weight above. New piers and arches were
in the several openings, and under the front and back
he Terrace and of the houses in John Street. Piers
es were constructed under the two staircase walls of
ace houses, which formerly rested on the span of

twelve rooms with a gallery, an the interior walls of which has
now been renewed or repaired. The brickwork of the fro
wall of the Terrace above the great arches from the top
the piers up iron railing, being very unsound, was c
out from 14 8 in. in depth, and renewed in cemen
The piers w red and strengthened, new cement ca

VIEW AT CORNER OF ADELPHI TERRACE AND ADAM STREET.

Most of the parts for this   figure were
found by using parts of an old mincer, and some
sheet zinc left over from the pantry window.

Cut out, roll and glue the Body.
Glue the Legs into position,

first one side and then the other.

All confusion will be avoided,

The mighty gulf which separates us
The difficulty of the task

your filthiness

Civil Servant

She actioned a lover from polystyrene packaging,
  newspaper and an old leotard.
Unfortunately she could never get him
to really give a shit. He was handsome enough,
and had an aptitude for handshakes
and grilling fish, but it turns out
that isn't enough to sustain a relationship.

Artist

She created a lover from failure
  and scraps of coloured paper.
What a man that was!
He swore in ten languages,
had large bollocks,
was as as keen and heartless as his kin:
the wind in the trees.

extravagant and luxurious fêtes
softly over her buttocks;
it is well to do this carefully
inwardly she was a hollow sham.
looking   for mere romance

"It's like a nightmare—where every-
thing you touch turns into a hat!" she
sighed.

Teaching Assistant

She fashioned a lover from silk gloves,
  a home-brew kit and a tweed waistcoat.
He was briefly a laugh but in the long-term
a prattish buffoon. Her flatmates took
his component parts to the charity shop
while she was at work.
It was better for everyone.

Shop Manager

She arranged a lover from Tupperware,
a pillow pack of coriander, and a pair
  of laboriously made acrylic pom-poms.
Quel surprise
he wasn't interested in females.
An epic lover though.

Therapist

She assembled a lover from her late husband's
blue puffa jacket, an ordnance survey map
  and a bleak disco night buried in her adolescence.
He was young and strong and amazingly innocent.
  What is my name? he asked.
  I'm too tired to start at the beginning like this,
she sighed, *I'll be dead soon.*
  No! he shouted, *impossible!*
Let me save you, you're all I have!

Estate Agent

She boasted a lover from an oak floorboard
  and the property section of the local paper.
He was small and sported a fine period moustache
though he saw himself as large and imposing,
priding himself on his many original features.
The thought of kids absolutely demolished him
as he stood night after night
overlooking their immaculate lawn.

  In the end she ran off with a lover
she drew on the back of an envelope
who came with planning permission.

Investment Banker

She shuffled a lover from two hundred euros
  and the smack of the lido on an icy morning,
he rose glowing from the water
with shoulders so wide it took her half an hour
to scan the full breadth of his manliness
  You'll do, she said, clicking her teeth.
  I have no papers, he admitted,
  I'll sort that out, she beamed,
*I'm a genius at bureaucracy
and also, I have access to funds.*

Vitznau mit Park-Hotel gegen den Schwalmis

Vitznau: le Park-Hôtel et le Schwalmis

Vitznau: Park Hotel, looking towards the Schwalmis

Vitznau: il Park-Hotel verso lo Schwalmis

Farmer

She cultivated a lover from spring rain,
   silage and an old scythe.
Demeter had a real nose for the weather
and loved to rise early
mending the ice bucket
of a cold dawn
to the jazz of *cock a doodle do*
and the buttered toast of a hot dream.

Lab Technician

She developed a lover from an almost empty
blister pack of paracetamol
   and all the random keys. Not promising?
In fact, he was so finely attuned to her
it was like she'd finally found
her own front door.

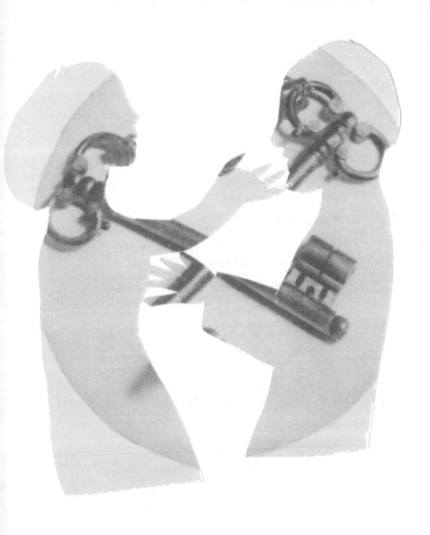

Betty felt as if she was in a fairy world

floor after floor of anonymous shut doors

Theorist

She summoned a lover from chewing gum blobs,
cigarette ends and a torn copy of Sartre's
  Les Mouches.
She smuggled him into the cinema
where they chewed every flicker out of
  the darkness.
When they emerged six weeks later
it was still raining. She couldn't begin
to explain what she'd been up to
no, she could not.

vous
80
sabots, verni et Daim
bottes chevreau,
Hautes bottes Daim,
bottes
Satin noir
or et

summer

Cruise Ship Dancer

She manifested a lover from a pair
  of pillowslips and a fire extinguisher,
his speciality was tango but tbh
he was versatile.
He was paranoid though
about not being real
and slept lightly for fear
that she'd throw him overboard
when the passion dimmed.

Architect

She structured a lover from a set square,
  her late grandfather's binoculars and some fudge,
he towered over her with a gentle smile.
They went on holiday at once,
first to Las Vegas and then to a huge
totally undeveloped marshland
where the only buildings were nests.

ARCHITECTS HAVE USED AND RECOMMENDED

fine sheer black stockings and a short corset

Telegrams: Eternity, Phone, London

Vicar

She channelled a lover from twigs
   and a handful of gold sequins: *Durga manifest!*
Copper-skinned and ten-armed in full trance
she dropped her weapons and threw herself
into their embrace. The quadruple slide
of such bosoms together created a new religion
that the world would be mad about if it knew.

touch not the unclean *thing*

Scissors are the first essential,

Now you can model it

There is su

akes, fruit, hams, pies,

de range of glues available,

there shall be no more curse :

in the new mood

Nurse

She melded a lover from her broken watch
    and Ken from Barbie and Ken.
He relished his new life on the dream pillow
of a flesh and blood woman. He listened
to her stories of war in the Congo
and offered one platitude after another.
She just let these drift over her
she found his monotony soothing.

Ceramicist

She patted a lover from clay beads
  and refill pads.
Day after day
she lay on him weeping,
which slowly smoothed him
and watered the camomile
that burst from his cracks.
  They mended each other,
the street and the city,
sleeping the urban bluster
into a peace
akin to unfired bowls
stacked on a silent shelf.

Kickboxer

She jump-started a lover from rubber bands,
    a bollard and plenty of hard cash,
he was exhausting and extreme.
When she went home to Slovakia
she left him asleep in a public park.
Once back in the UK
she threw herself into her sport.

Wade found the LeBlanc house's bathtub and sink on the roadside after Hurricane Katrina. He designed the shelf next to the tub from a plank of salvaged tupelo wood

Data Analyst

She tabled a lover from a rustic pickle,
a universally popular sauce
  and several customer responses.
His apparent bonhomie
masked his Machiavellian nature.
At first he met her every need
then one day he just upped and left
having first hacked and emptied
her bank account
and erased all her contacts.
She hasn't used her imagination since.

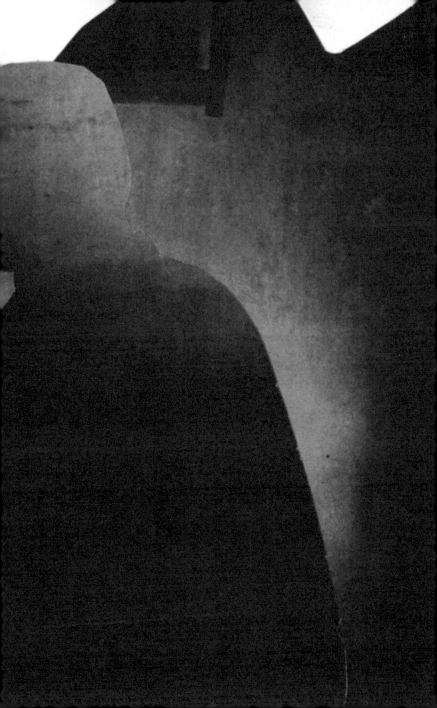

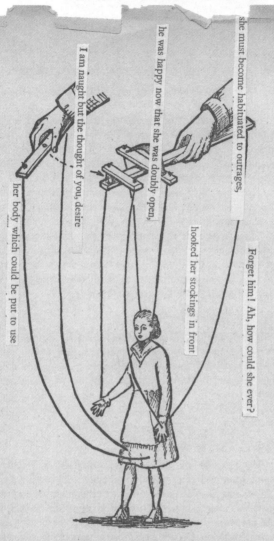

she must become habituated to outrages,

he was happy now that she was doubly open,

I am naught but the thought of you, desire

her body which could be put to use

hooked her stockings in front

Forget him! Ah, how could she ever?

Strings are attached in this manner.

19

Actor

She conjured a lover from a borrowed copy
of The Scottish Play, a highlighter pen
  and some sugar-free wheat-free granola.
He turned out to be in love with somebody else
who was in turn in love with somebody else
who was debating whether to leave his
wife and children.
  I was hoping for some let up from reality,
she sighed, *how typically ghastly,*
how authentically painful
even my own script turns out to be.

Quantity Surveyor

She sorted a lover from rich tea biscuits
  and insulation tape, he hummed little tunes
in the office where no one else
could see him. He lived for her firm voice
on the phone bringing builders into line,
he guessed it was easier to be him than her
though he was all too aware
of his transience.

Pastry People

't pastry

ı:

ɔn a lightly floured working top.

: the pastry into sections, one for ea
ɪ. Flatten the pastry into different figu.
er, mother and 2 children.

can also make your pets.

ʌur mother to cook them for t

Jazz Trumpeter

She arranged a lover
from a torn
magazine
and a small stash of weed.
He'd float by and catch her
in the satin-clad
small hours
they'd devil the standards
with hot licks and
schmaltz
  my
how they'd
improvise.

Zoo Keeper

She papier machéd a lover
from *Your Guide to the Zoo*
made into tough pulp
  with macaw and penguin guano.
They were as uncomplaining as a whelk
but their other attributes
were fully mammalian,
they liked playing feeding time and "cages"
long after the visitors had left.

Art Gallery Attendant

She sweet-talked a lover from concrete,
  glass and steel.
He shone like the entitled,
was never soft
but sometimes sympathetic,
as someone whose opinions are echoed
all over town can afford to be.

Hairdresser

She teased a lover from Earl Grey tea bags,
  an old laptop and those strawberry shoelaces.
She trained him to cut, curl and colour her hair.
They bought a pair of poodles
and used them to win competitions,
their rainbow-fluff treatment
took America by storm.
Looking like a poodle was the new pressure.

Mary was a great one for lists and
plans, be it said. Feeling very business-
like, she sat down at her mother's desk

6. Draw a face on the head. Colour with paints (Fig. 2).

Head of Human Resources

She bantered a lover from cracker jokes,
  dental floss and a four colour biro,
they got on famously.
It was only two years
into their subsequent marriage
she noticed with a sinking feeling
  Oh God, he's exactly like my Dad!

62

Non begin:

Place a button in the ce
ric over it, so that you
togram). Wind a
wrapped button; tie a kno... so that it c...
'mly into the clou... knotting. Tie
Tie peas f... 'nnot possibly come undone. Tie
that it c... ne way at the four corners. Now
'h in the sa... 'et of cold dye an... 'ave for 30
'o the buc... out, rinse it wel...
'n... 'ou take it...
'mi... 'en all your v.rappings. H
tap, ti...
v, and ask your mother to iro...

y held in its
y fe...

e cloth out

ushrooms; Mont.
'eir particul...
enne
'spc
o e...
which include *casareccí*, a sc...
ravioli stuffed with choc...
ugared, doughnut-shan...
ost notable culin...
e. The town o'
gh the power of...
air, and Federig...
'oino, was afraid of poison: he had all his dishes
'oning because it was harder to i... 'nate

o an unseas... 'd dish. But the duke, as fond of seaso... as
ristocrat, had his own sauce—prepared for him at the _____ by
'd servant from secret ingredients, and ladled on to the dishes when they
'h been judged safe to eat. A few years ago a playw... ',
"search for an historical play, cam..."
"'in... 'it, and found it so..."

Pattern Cutter

She pressed a lover from table salt,
bias binding and a string of rosary beads
inherited from an aunt. The aunt's ghost
haunted their lovemaking. Christ it was creepy!
    Fuck you! she shouted out of the window
as he slunk off to make a pilgrimage
somewhere on the other side of the world.

I watched her in her bitterness, so
young, climbing up the stairs.
. 'She'll be much better,' said Anne-Marie, a
        In any case you are obviously
rather too old for childbearing.

Pop singer

She blossomed a lover from headphones,
sugar mice and the patterned tights her
  cousin gave her for her birthday.
He was basically quite a lazy moper.
She ditched him at a festival
but was sorry when she heard
he'd stopped breathing the next day.
It turned out he really needed her.

Engineer

She created a lover from melamine, sellotape
  and yesterday's spaghetti.
  Who... who.. are you? he spluttered
as he juddered to life
in her salty little hands.
  I'm your girlfriend silly! she giggled
high on sudden power.

My dear, you've worked marvels!

Fitness Instructor

She bossed a lover from grass clippings,
  some resistance bands, and a shell ornament,
he wouldn't speak.
They got by on continental glances they shot
each other across her breakfast bar in Burnley.
  It'll be worth it in the end, she thought
no stranger to positive goal setting.

With the scissors c
4 ft long by 2 in. de
Measure the size of
Place the string on t
join it to make
ou wish, pain
he feath
to

la the fea
sive tape a
d side (Fig
hing
feathe.

nem.
ed cardboard,
largest for the

on its side and
the back of the

lown in a ta

will do fine

74

ene

or yogurt pots, scouring powder, poster

for   g small autumn bulbs or
y flowers, one in each place.

A piece of burnt cork

Try to look forward, not back, and
realize that true happiness never comes

Politician

She manifested a lover from violent unrest
  naked ambition and an old 60 watt lightbulb.
She dressed him up so fine
even she believed he was real
but he gave the game away
every time he opened his mouth
  We really care, he boomed
sounding nothing like a human.
Turned out he was harder to get rid of
than a plastic nappy on a beach.

she took the head out of the bag,

somewhat firm, lightly browned but pink inside.

Seems some unfortunate housing official
got himself manhandled

Lingerie Designer

She twisted a lover from knicker elastic
  a bad attitude and nicotine
let me tell you he was a lot of fun
let me tell you he was all over her
like the proverbial,
more itchy than the proverbial
because they sweated it out
in slimy nylon smalls
revelled in the squeak of their flesh
on the sun baked vinyl
of her American diner themed banquettes
  Oh oh marry me! he blurted, in thrall
to her chutzpah and feather trim.
Did I mention he was rash?

She had a strange, excited, light-headed feeling.

I am as empty as a hole in a stocking.

You should speak to your doctor about it—he is far too accustomed to dealing with complaints of this kind for you to feel embarrassed.

Conservationist

She dreamt up a lover from fallen leaves
   and porridge oats, he was big and beardy
and falling into him was like falling into bracken.
They hummed themselves a treehouse
from Schubert lieder and secondhand books
and holed up against every one
of these so called winters.

Dressing up in newspaper is a good way

to spend a wet afternoon.

Primary School Teacher

She crafted a lover from panty liners,
  parking meters and loyalty cards,
after all, it was time she settled down.
She was just getting the hang of him
when he announced he was leaving her
for a friend she'd made only a few days before
from pine needles, sandwich spread
and a Beefeater gin miniature.
   Well I hope you're happy together, she snarled,
banging the door of the fridge.

Going into the kitchen, Mary got out the meat for lunch. There were a lot of cold potatoes, she noticed. Why not make rissoles?

and so on, alternating until everyone is exhausted.

there is a terrible secret

the girls sat petrified

someone had carelessly splattered diamonds

the breath came into them

You left these, Eve, you chump

unlucky waterhen

burnt as a witch.

89

Anaesthetist

She stitched together a lover from post-
  operative discard:
organs and extrusions
and an eagle's feather stolen
  off an Apache war bonnet.
As he came to he was furious,
then he laughed.
   Why should I look at my painful history
when you have given me a future?
He flexed his arms
from shoulder to finger tip.
The masectomised breasts
stitched decoratively all over his torso
rose and fell like inflatable fish scales
   Am I such a curiosity? he asked.
   You are perfect, said the anaesthetist,
and she meant it.

Upholsterer

She crafted a lover from 5 yds plum velvet,
  a book of ballads and a shovel of loose leaf tea.
He had large lustrous eyes and a corpulence
you see stuffed into tailoring only in
  period dramas.
His mournful devotion ornamented
her parlour but briefly
as he declined to accompany her
to her next more minimal phase.
His tears were Victorian crystal.

is a single-storey extension across the back of the
n five french windows onto the garden. The stone
8th-century, reclaimed from a church, and the same
polished to a mirror sheen, has been used for the work
surfaces. The giant armoire is a copy of an antique, and houses the
television, as well as a collection of large-scale blue-and-white pots

Garden Designer

She drew up a lover from sherbet lemons,
  a couple of HB pencils and a scouring pad,
they had hours of fun on the kitchen table.
She was hurt when she overheard him
describing their relationship as 'doodling'.
    Doodling! Doodling?
He'll be getting me an adult
colouring book next!

Nail Technician

She wafted a lover from shellac,
  Bovril and broken paving slabs,
he found it hard to concentrate.
She'd scratch him awake
as he smiled in dreams of beef castles
with ten turrets and pink flags.
They lounged together
in a mildly hallucinogenic cloud.

do I seek to please men?

Don't you long to have one *now*?

If you have made it too wet add more flour.

Investigative Journalist

She compiled a lover from clothes pegs, lipsalve
and a roll of film leftover from her 35mm days.
He appeared suave but as an actual guy
he was somewhat stilted.
She introduced him to Match of the Day,
  which helped
or maybe she just got used to
and learnt to love his awkwardness.

Librarian

She composed a lover from the dismantled
workings of a record player
and the middle hundred pages
  of a rarely borrowed novel.
He was endearingly weak
as he blinked into the sunlit wooden interior.
  All these years I've waited, he marvelled,
and finally I've witnessed it for myself
true love exists outside fiction!
The librarian shrugged,
  Who says we're not fictional?
She too was pretty excited
only she'd trained herself
NEVER TO SHOW IT.

south, features a bench by James Moore
nsole tables holding busts of the fourth
s Fox. A 17th-century cabinet at the end is
ortoiseshell and fitted intricately with
his room is used for the Raynham Recitals

Mealtime Supervisor

She dished up a lover from stiff mash,
  a lanyard, lard and gravy.
They were a comfort at first
then she noticed their blandness.
First it exasperated her,
then it threatened to suffocate her.
   Why are you yelling? they said,
calm yet sinister,
you wanted someone
old fashioned and reliable, did you not?

Charity Volunteer

She assembled a lover from goji berries,
  a moth-eaten pashmina and milk bottle tops,
he was an easy target.
They folded into each other's mustiness
with relief - the real people she met
were often so jaded.

                    .s
  ₂.   .nish₁
  hei   .light inc
    e   gnity. It il'   ₁
      's   ner calmne   ec
          u.y and j-   n.
  guesses at than perceives ..   rc.
  when René informed her that h.   .aving, nigh.
  .ready fallen. O was naked in her ce. waiting to be led
he refectory. For his part, her lover was dressed as usual, i.
he suit he wore everyday in town. When he'd taken her in hi
irms the rough tweed of his coat had chafed her nipples. He
:issed her, lay her upon the bed, lay down beside her, his face
o her face, and tenderly and slowly and gently he took her
  oving to and fro now in this, now j the other of the tw
    :sages offered to him, finally spillir   -elf into her mo
      -h, when he was done, he kisse-
        -ore I go I'd -

Waitress

She fashioned a lover from stacked up DVDs
  of teen flicks and rom-coms,
he was decidedly unstable.
He licked the gravy off his plate
in front of her mother.
It was nothing like in the movies
it was absolutely revolting.

Events Manager

She magicked a lover at sunset
from a pile of white china plates and a
  crow's feather,
he appeared in a white suit with a black shirt
and a pink tie and said: *Shall we dance?*
For him, formal dancing was a compulsory prelude
to any thoughts of romance.
I believe they are waltzing still.

Film Maker

She storyboarded a lover from a discount wig
and some illegal firearms,
you'll never guess what happened next
it was awful — people died —
but it was huge at the box office.

Fashion Vlogger

She scribbled a lover from hair clips,
  peanut butter and safety matches,
a tall American stood before her with a bland smile.
  Let me try again, she said.
  Oh no you don't little missy, he said
from behind mirrored sunglasses.
He picked her up and locked her in her bedroom,
she heard the front door slam
then a familiar growl: the ignition of
her own cherry-red fiat!
Its roar fading, then silence.

Doctor

She fangled a lover from get well soon cards
  and some vinyl examination gloves,
he was an utter dreamboat
and insisted on days off,
box sets and date nights.
It couldn't last.
  We want different things,
she admitted from her booth
of medicinal sadness.

Five Stones

If one day you have no companion, find five small pebbles
play five stones. It is one of the oldest games recorded – it
...ayed by the Gr...ks – and you can play it anywhere. It is

...ve evenly matched carpal bones
... but fiv... ...all pebbles or shel

Any number of playe...
One player chooses a long word like DISAPPOINTMENT, ...
down on a piece of paper and numbers each letter. Then he tells
the other players how many letters the word has, so that they can
make and numb...
...ny dashes on their paper.
...t the others can work out his word.
...will see it is often made up

...and pencil each

◄ **RECOVERED VICTIM** of 1953 heart attack, Ka Topka, wears apparatus to measure physical suit bility for his job at Cleveland Graphite Bronze C

N OF E... ...hows relation to electroga... ...raph, loads manure while ...ng
Here Purdue breathing-a... ...tus. Study will enable doc... ...o
...gelsang, wired advise farm... ...n work he can do after heart atta...

79

A stuffed French fight
mself by the drawing
antique chimney pi
nb's 'Oxford' design
twood mirror above i
n Newhailes House

Taxidermist

She scraped together a lover from excess fur,
  staples and her piled up takeaway coffee cups.
He was a sardonic fellow who could
whistle all the hits of the Sixties.
They shared the exhilarating shock,
that undeniable daily shock
of being alive.
  They drank each other up
with the moist glass eyes
of the grateful.

untold hours of pleasure,
values of the work. F   th
' like to have, but   are
 king them. Once y
 ...s of simple ba...
 ity will open the way to

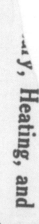

..ry, Heating, and

SPECIALISTS in every SANITARY

including **STERIL...**

and other **SP...**

INFI...

COMPL...

Hot

Plumber

She gushed a lover from accumulated
plughole gunk, a hot tap, and a dirty secret
  she'd kept since school.
He worshipped her porcelain skin
and her practicality
he had a thing about cleanliness -
so they mostly had sex in the shower,
or at least, after she'd let him
scrub, polish, ornament and perfume
every intricate part of her.

Weaver

She clicked a lover from natural pigment dyed wool
  and some lonely days in the mountains,
He smiled sideways, the cheeky goat,
he made adventurousness routine
    You aren't lonely any more are you? he grinned
as again he tied her to the bed with her own yarn,
and set about her warp and weft
as if he was born to such a task.

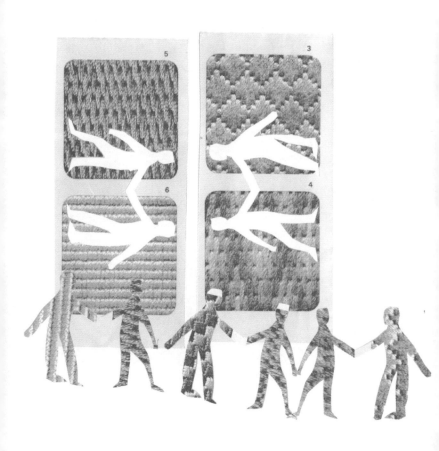

Porn Star

She whipped up a lover from rubber,
  treacle and iron chains,
the relief being that neither was
interested in sex.
They liked to make a fuss
of their cat Venus, watch documentaries
and try out new recipes off the internet.

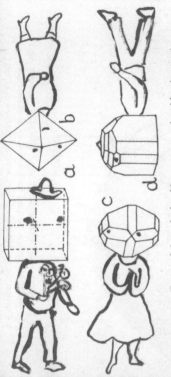

FIG. 4.—Forms of the orthorhombic system. a, prism (showing axes). b, bi-pyramid. c, combination of forms. d, crystal of topaz

placed base to base (also called the TRIMETRIC system) (fig. 4).

Gems which crystallize in the orthorhombic system are :

Andalusite.	Aragonite.	Beryllonite.
Bronzite.	Chrysoberyl.	Danburite.
Dumortierite.	Enstatite.	Fibrolite.
Hambergite.	Hypersthene.	Iolite.
Kornerupine.	Marcasite.	Peridot.
Prehnite.	Staurolite.	Thomsonite.
Topaz.	Variscite.	Zoisite.

THE MONOCLINIC SYSTEM has three axes, all of unequal length, two of which are at right angles to each other and the third inclined. One axis is placed vertically and of the

Your hostess should open the door.

There are usually plenty of nuts about

'What an odd way to behave,

Prove that you are

sensible and grown-up by accepting facts and fitting in

Bookkeeper

She whittled a lover from a discarded
  tennis racket,
a packet of salt and vinegar crisps and a
  road-kill fox.
  Mmm, there is something rugged about him!
smiled her friend Sue.
He was refreshingly open and frank with her,
yet guarded and jealous with Sue and Jeff.
  Why do you even bother with those idiots?
he muttered.

Graphic Novelist

She drafted a lover from yards
of loo paper and five fitful petals
trailing in the wake of last weeks
  stale bouquet.
He almost passed out
at the fragrant silk of her skin
and fell upon her
with shocking heaviness.
Afterwards he shook with grief
or was it relief?
His tears almost flooded
her shoebox apartment.

Optician

She scored a lover from lidless felt-tips
  and last night's Indian takeaway,
he was a bit of a know-it-all and she wondered
if she'd inadvertently manifested Siri.
She kept trying to chuck him
but her friends liked him
and he came into his own on quiz night.

Yoga Teacher

She created a lover from spare denim
 and a cat scratching post.
He was awesome at headstands,
bouncy as the heather on Dartmoor,
breezy as a mom in a '70s sitcom,
but ultimately as cold
as the Linda McCartney sausages
in her freezer. *Om shanti shanti!*

Physicist

She tabled a lover from icing sugar,
  a barometer and an obscure stringed instrument,
he was Pegasus-like, defying gravity.
They soared all over the cosmos
moaning and melting.
  Where the hell have you been?
asked her extremely suspicious sister.
  Oh nowhere, she sighed,
tapping the telltale snow
off her hard to conceal
recently sprouted wings.

Einsiedeln; Stiftskirche, Chor, Hochaltar

Einsiedeln; the Choir and Altar

Einsiedeln; L'Eglise Collégiale, Chœur et Grand Autel

Chiesa Collegiale di Einsiedeln; coro, altare maggiore

Social Worker

She magicked a lover from a fridge magnet
  and a firing squad,
she stood in front of him
but he missed every time.
It was like he did it on purpose.
   Look at me, she insisted
aim for my heart!
   I can't, he stuttered, *I, I love you, but*
as a stranger loves
a daisy in the park.

Sous Chef

She rustled up a lover from tahini,
pomegranate molasses, a favourite page
  from Alice B. Toklas and a squeeze of lemon.
At the end of her shift
she'd give her a piggyback home
where they'd lick the accumulated sauces
off each others' secret recipes
then lie as naked as dumplings in a steamer.

Her heart began to thump

flushed with pleasure

like butter

like

heaped up silver

the invisible

EXCITING

ELECTRIC

nothing

Firefighter

She plucked a lover from green baize
  and a rain-warped pack of playing cards,
he was devastatingly good looking.
She tried to find the courage to address him
but he evaporated like a fortune
amassed over several generations
and spent in one afternoon.

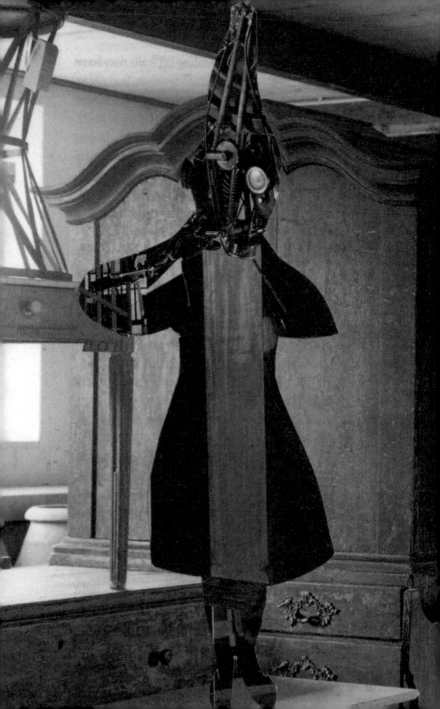

Receptionist

She typed up a lover from a frayed
  courier bag and a desk diary,
he was classic husband material.
At weekends they'd take off on bikes
with breaks in pubs they'd researched online.
He was as weak for a roast as she was.

147

Writer

She swooned herself a lover from a dictionary
   and a courgette.
   You're great, you entertain yourself
and sometimes you entertain me, she said.
   I don't feel so great, he said, and booked
to see a vegetable counsellor.
   It's like my head and my body
are totally separate.

A free-standing figure is a considerable advance
a body is easily produced, but heads can be a stumbling block

UNHAPPINESS very rarely endures
unless it is carefully nursed.

it lay desolate

scum on the water,

in the lips of talkers,

s decent but humble

PEACE

in England,

---

4. If you want a girl doll, leave her as she is (Fig. 5).
5. To make a boy doll, tie the wool once more to lengthen the body, then divide and tie for legs (Fig. 3).

Researcher

She conjured a lover from
a battalion of earwigs,
  paperclips and cheese.
After half an hour of muted screaming
she vowed never to go into that room again.
   What was I thinking of?
Her friend shrugged,
   We all do embarrassing things
when we're desperate.

Archeologist

She moulded a lover from mud
  and a fragment of smoky Roman glass.
He was tougher than your modern bloke
and they marched into a shared future
in a straight line
in all weathers.
He taught her Latin
and that's what they spoke at home.
He laughed in the face of Death,
and Climate Change
  Amor Vincit Omnia, he said,
Hey! I'm the proof.

Dentist

She polished a lover from a shattered mirror
  and a broken string of pearls.
The lover was a small dark woman
who straightaway asked,
  Do you love yourself? then,
Do you believe in Luck, good or bad?
  I'm... I'm not sure... stuttered the dentist.
  Well I'm your Lucky Day, smiled the lover
mending the necklace and the mirror
with one easy hand wafting gesture
then planting on the dentist's mouth
a perfect ripe plum of a kiss.

we groan, earnestly desiring

filthiness of the flesh

love unfeigned,

Don't think me awful!

Index

Rare HOMAGE

ACKNOWLEDGMENTS

"Put me down and listen, you big oaf,"

I appreciate and value the   heavenly cloud of loveliness,

romantic castles and palaces

thank you,

I am indeed grateful for the valuable   sparkling   advice of friends

glorious other artists,

and artistic contemporaries.

Incredible   TREASURES
serious thinking
poets of national repute.

useful and artistic

EXTREMELY VALUABLE

they're Sans Egal.

All you need is: large newspapers, pins, a friend. integrity
and common sense are useful attributes.

We've got a date for the Palais. Let's go.

Acknowledgements

Thanks to all the lovers, real and imaginary, dead or alive.
Thanks to my brilliant encouraging friends.
Thanks to all my wonderful family, in particular Adam, Rosa and
Conrad, who keep my feet on the ground, supposing there is any.

This book has come into being with help from the following:
Alison Winch who is a mensch.
David and Ping Henningham who offered to publish it
straightaway, and then collaborated with such vision.
The Hawthornden Fellowship for a fully supported
writing month.
Peter Beardsley and Thomas Dane for that peaceful space to
work in near Conrad's college.
Joan Hecktermann for the mountain of collage gold.
Gemma Seltzer, and all the generous supporters who pledged
money for this production on Kickstarter.

THANK YOU
Sophie Herxheimer, Brixton, July 2019

Wandering Barques

This book was made possible by the following backers:

Ken Grady • Chris Winter • Sophie Henderson
Manya and Alex • Tamar Yoseloff • John Stuttle
Jeremy O'Sullivan • Greg and Ginger Burrell • Marion
Hysteria Clevercloggs • Alison Winch

Peter J. King • Anna Blasiak • Fiona Larkin • Sarah Campbell
Alice Leach • Frances • Zoë Burt • Susan R Grossman • Sue
Ian Chung • Roz Symon • Gwen Rahardja • Selene • Therese
Anderberg • Kelly • Nancy Campbell • Julia Bird • Sarah Alice
Cave • Desdemona Mccannon • Deborah Alma • Victoria Tyler
Jo Raphael • Edward Venning • Fr Justin Gau • Stuart
Charlesworth • Sarah Salway • Katrina Naomi • Derek
Harper • Pam • Kathy Pimlott • Shauna Darling Robertson
Gemma Seltzer • Amy Goodwin • Sam Jordison • Helen Bowell
Tom Jenks • Manda Glanfield • Claire Collison • Mel Pryor
Jessica Harby • Charlotte Herxheimer • Christine Herxheimer
Emily Haworth-Booth • Lucy Dallas Brett • Alice Hiller
Elfego Baca • Nate Merchant • Jacqueline Saphra
Martin Grover • Barbara Del Mercato

We also thank our anonymous supporters.

Henningham Family Press

Find more of our publications at:
henninghamfamilypress.co.uk

All our paperback fiction is reinterpreted in our studio with the author, as limited edition handmade artists' books.

By the same author:

The Listening Forest

Your Candle Accompanies The Sun:
My homage to Emily Dickinson

HENNINGHAM
FAMILY
PRESS

About the Author

Sophie Herxheimer is an artist and poet. Recent books include *The Listening Forest*, *Your Candle Accompanies the Sun* (Henningham Family Press) and *The Practical Visionary* with Chris McCabe (Hercules Editions).

Velkom to Inklandt (Short Books, 2017) was an Observer book of the month and a Sunday Times book of the year.

Her work has been anthologised in *The New Concrete*, (2015, ed. Victoria Bean, Chris McCabe, Hayward Publishing) and *Ways of Drawing* (ed. Julian Bell, Thames and Hudson 2019).

Her commissions include a 300m hand-printed tablecloth that ran the length of Southwark Bridge for a public banquet, a 48m Margate seafront hoarding that featured food stories drawn with local people, and portraits of 30 influential poets for the Poetry Foundation in Chicago.

Her work has been exhibited in The National Portrait Gallery and Tate Modern, and a wall of her story drawings made in collaboration with a community in Liverpool is installed in The Museum of Liverpool until 2022.

She has held residencies for LIFT, Transport for London, The Migration Museum and National Poetry Day. In 2019 she was the recipient of a Hawthornden Fellowship.